P9-CEJ-903

The Easy and Relaxing

MEMORY

Activity Book for Adults

By J.D. Kinnest

Includes Relaxing Memory Activities, Easy Puzzles, Brain Games and More

LOMIC BOOKS

The Easy and Relaxing **MEMORY** Activity Book for Adults

By J.D. Kinnest

ISBN: 978-1-988923-18-5
Published by Lomic Books
Kitchener, Ontario

Copyright

Puzzles and text are copyright © 2020-2021 Lomic Books
Images in this book, and on the cover, are either public domain, images from pixabay.com used under the Pixabay License (2020), or licensed from vectorstock.com — some of which have been adapted by Lomic Books
Cover design is copyright © 2020 Lomic Books

Disclaimer

The puzzles, games and activities in this book are for entertainment purposes only. Although the author and publisher have worked very hard to ensure that the information in this book is accurate, the reader should be aware that errors and/or omissions may occur. The author and publisher disclaim any liability to any person or party for any loss resulting from reliance on any information in this book.

Table of Contents

Table of contents continued...

Introduction

Welcome to *The Easy and Relaxing Memory Activity Book for Adults!*

This book is filled with fun and entertaining activities that are designed to give your memory a pleasant workout.

You will find a terrific variety of activities that exercise short-term memory, long-term recall and other mental skills.

Short-term Memory

You can have fun exercising your short-term memory with several enjoyable activities including:

- **Delightful Details**: In this game, you memorize a picture, then turn the page, and fill in the missing detail in an almost identical picture.

- **Particular Pictures:** You memorize three pictures in this memory game. Then pick out the pictures from a selection of images.

- **Backwards:** In this memory activity, the goal is to write sentences, that are based on the section's theme, backwards.

- **Silly Sentences:** This memory activity has a fun sentence which you memorize; and then you pick out the correct sentence from four options.

- **Terrific Lists:** You memorize a short related list of six items in this game. Then you pick out the items from a grid of words related to the theme.

- **Memory Challenge:** In this memory game, there is a short list of unrelated words that you memorize, and then write down on the next page.

These entertaining memory games provide a fun and relaxing way to exercise your short-term memory.

Long-term Memory

You can have fun exercising your long-term memory with several fun activities in this book, including:

- **Cool Categories:** In this long-term memory game, write down as many items you can come up with that belong in a specific category.

- **Starts With:** The goal of this memory game is to recall specific words from the clues that are provided.

- **Lovely Memories:** Write about some of your favorite memories or experiences to help exercise your long-term recall.

- **Complete It!:** In this long-term memory game, you fill in the missing word in famous sayings or titles.

These long-term memory games provide a great way to exercise your long-term recall.

Classic Puzzles & Brain Games

In addition to all of the great memory games, this book has many classic puzzles and brain games. These puzzles provide extra variety and mental exercise. Theses puzzles include:

- **Word Search**
- **Sudoku**
- **Odd One Out**

- **Two of a Kind**
- **Well Made Words**
- **Find the Differences**

Altogether, this book provides an easy and fun way to exercise short-term memory, long-term recall and other mental skills.

We hope you will have hours of fun and entertainment.

Enjoy!

Memory Activities, Puzzles, and Brain Games

Around the ❧ House ❧

Includes Delightful Details, Starts With, Cool Categories, Particular Pictures, Lovely Memories, Backwards, Terrific Lists, Word Search, Sudoku, Find the Differences, Silly Sentences, Odd One Out, Merry Matching, and The Memory Challenge

Starts with "S"

In this memory puzzle, the answer to each clue begins with the letter "S" and relates to this section's theme of 'Around the House.'

1. Comfortable place to sit, most often with arms and a back.

2. Used to dig around in the backyard or in the garden.

3. Convenient place to wash food and clean dishes.

4. Often stored in the closet, it helps transport clothing.

5. Takes you from one level of a house to another.

6. Place to store books, or display ornamental objects.

7. A place for a person to wash, that's faster than taking a bath.

8. Kitchen chair that usually has no back and three legs.

Solution on page 134

PARTICULAR PICTURES

Take a look at the three kitchen items below. Take your time to memorize the items. Then turn the page and pick out the items that you memorized.

Turn the page to continue

PARTICULAR PICTURES..... CONTINUED

Did you study the three items on the previous page? Great! Now circle the three kitchen items that you memorized.

Silly Sentences...

Take some time to memorize the silly sentence below. Then pick it out from a selection of four similar sentences on the next page. Then repeat for the second silly sentence!

Sentence One:

"Larry loves to relax in
his living room."

turn the page ➤

Sentence Two:

"Sara sips her tea while
singing a song."

turn the page ➤

This puzzle continues from the previous page.

SILLY SENTENCES..... CONTINUED

Sentence One:

Pick the silly sentence you memorized on the previous page from the four options below.

A) Larry loves to eat in his living room

B) Larry loves to relax in his living room.

C) Larry hates to relax in his living room.

D) Larry loves to relax in his bedroom.

....

Sentence Two:

Pick the silly sentence you memorized on the previous page from the four options below.

A) Sandra sips her soda while singing a song.

B) Sarah drinks her coffee while singing a song.

C) Sarah sips her tea while humming a song.

D) Sarah sips her tea while singing a song.

Solution on page 134

Delightful Details

Take a look at the picture of the lady below. On the next page is an identical picture, that is missing two details. When you are ready, turn the page and fill in the missing details.

Time To Cook!

Turn the page to continue

This puzzle continues from the previous page.

Delightful Details... *continued*

Have you studied the lady on the previous page? Excellent! Now draw in the two details that will make the lady below identical to the image on the previous page.

FIND THE 5 DIFFERENCES

Find the 5 differences between the two men.

WORD SEARCH
UP IN THE ATTIC

In this classic puzzle, the goal is to find all the words listed below, within the letter grid on the right. Each word is placed in a straight line; either horizontally, vertically or diagonally in the grid.

WORD LIST:

JOISTS	RAFTERS	BOXES
SPACE	MEMORIES	LADDER
ROOM	STAIRS	DARK
SPIDERS	FILES	STUFF
FURNITURE	ROOF	UNFINISHED
SUITCASE	VENT	INSULATION
DECORATIONS	ART	STORE
SMALL	LADDER	WIRES
DINGY	GARRET	BOOKS
HATCH	MOLD	DUST
EXTRA	AWKWARD	LOFT

```
P F U R N I T U R E Q N G A I B R
M X R A F T E R S I J R X N H O Z
B Z A W K W A R D Q O X U Q S X U
R O G A R R E T M Y I J N F T E I
W I O J M R K Z M U S Y F I O S N
U Y F K V R V T X Q T I I L R C S
S Y T Q S L E W B N S I N E E J U
C H S P L D A R K L T D I S F K L
Q O A T A J O K O A M U S Y T Y A
N Y C T A E Q L F D D S H P E Y T
L S D Y C I I N X D E T E I X L I
S T O J J H R V N E B C D J T A O
P U W M E H V S J R C C I B R D N
I F I E G R F L L V P O H H A D C
D F R A E V U G S E J M O L D E H
E X E G D E S U A N L E P E J R Y
R A S R O O M T E T D I N G Y E W
S R I M D E C O R A T I O N S M L
E T S U I T C A S E Y X P J C Z O
Y B V D S E A R O O F L N T K Z F
U T V W C M E M O R I E S K D P T
Q S O U S P A C E Q J S M A L L C
```

SPOT THE ODD ONE OUT

Find the lamp that is different from the rest.

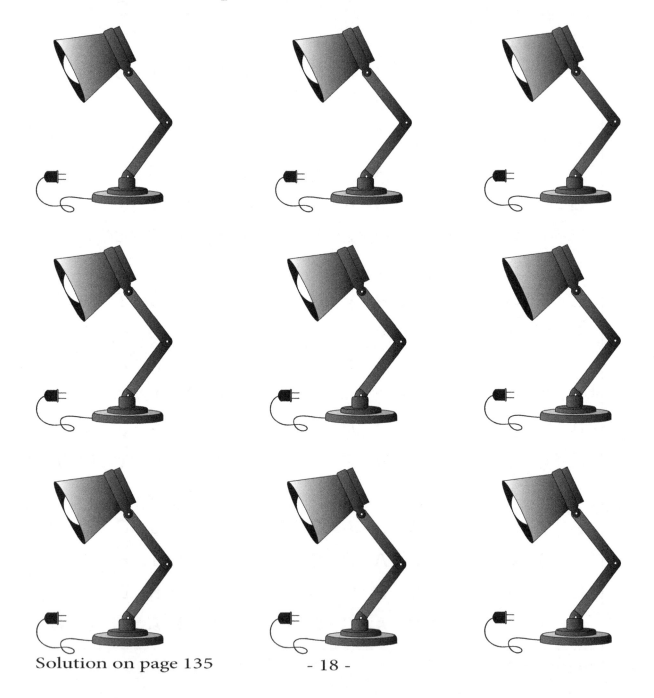

Solution on page 135

- 18 -

Cool Categories!

Make a list of items that are found on a living room wall. How many items can you think of?

1. _____
2. _____
3. _____
4. _____
5. _____
6. _____
7. _____
8. _____
9. _____
10. _____
11. _____
12. _____
13 _____
14. _____
15. _____
16. _____
17. _____
18. _____
19. _____
20. _____
21. _____

Make a list of the types of flooring you may find in a home. How many can you think of?

1. _____
2. _____
3. _____
4. _____
5. _____
6. _____
7. _____
8. _____
9. _____
10. _____
11. _____
12. _____
13 _____
14. _____
15. _____
16. _____
17. _____
18. _____
19. _____
20. _____
21. _____

Solution on page 135

Lovely Memories...

Describe in detail your childhood bedroom... If you had more then one childhood bedroom, pick your favorite. Try to recall interesting details including the color of the walls, displayed pictures, your bed, dresser, favorite toys and more.

_____

_____

_____

_____

_____

_____

_____

_____

_____

_____

_____

_____

_____

_____

_____

_____

_____

_____

_____

_____

_____

_____

_____

_____

_____

BACKWARDS SDRAWKCAB

In this activity, the goal is to write out the sentence backwards. To increase the level of difficulty of this memory challenge, you can minimize the number of times you refer to the original sentence.

1. The kitchen is the heart of the home.

Write it
backwards: _____

2. Make yourself comfortable.

Write it
backwards: _____

3. Let's gather by the fireplace.

Write it
backwards: _____

4. It's time for a nap!

Write it
backwards: _____

Solution on page 135   - 21 -

Complete It!
Famous Sayings

In this fun memory game, the goal is to fill in the missing word in each of the following popular sayings.

1. Don't cry over _____ milk.

2. Let sleeping _____ lie

3. Take with a _____ of salt.

4. Great minds _____ alike.

5. A leopard cannot _____ its spots.

6. Necessity is the _____ of invention.

7. One good turn _____ another.

8. The straw that _____ the camel's back.

9. Truth is _____ than fiction.

10. To _____ is human, to forgive divine.

Solution on page 136

MERRY MATCHING

How many times can you find this sequence of icons in a straight line in the grid below?

NOTE: The sequence of icons can be located vertically, diagonally, or horizontally in the gird. Also, the sequence of icons may be found forwards or backwards.

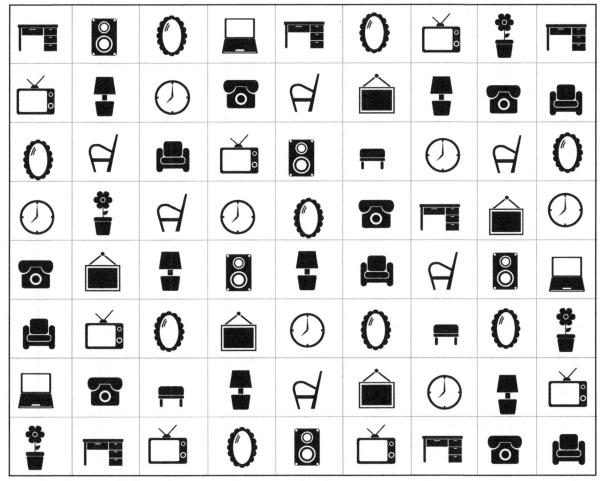

Solution on page 136

FUN WITH SUDOKU

In this brain game, the goal is to use the numbers 1 to 9 to fill in the grid below. In particular, there are three rules:

1. Each horizontal row needs to have the all of the numbers from 1 to 9, only once.

2. Each vertical row needs to have all the numbers from 1 to 9, only once.

3. Each 3 by 3 square has the numbers from 1 to 9, only once.

9		8	1	3	5	2	7	
1	5		7	4		3	6	9
	3	4		9	6		8	5
6	7	1	4	5	3		9	2
	8		9		2	4	1	7
	2	9	8		7	5	3	
8	1	7		2	4	9		3
2		5	3	7	1		4	8
3		6	5	8		7	2	1

Solution on page 136

Terrific Lists... Redecoration

In these puzzles, the goal is to memorize the list of items; and then turn the page and circle the items you remember.

Stacey is redecorating her bedroom. To the right is a list of items she wants to buy, so she can get started. Once you think you've memorized her list turn the page.

Stacey's List

lamp	hooks
paint	frame
blinds	blanket

turn the page

Max is redecorating his office. To the right is a list of items he wants to buy so he can get started. Once you think you've memorized Max's list turn the page.

Max's List

chair	basket
wallpaper	calendar
desk	rug

turn the page

These puzzles continue from the previous page.

Stacey's List

Circle each item on the right, which you remember from the Stacey's list (located on the previous page).

➡

ottoman	paint	bed
curtain	tapestry	blinds
lamp	bulb	shelf
pillow	throw	hangers
hooks	dresser	sconce
table	frame	tassels
throw	blanket	mirror

Max's List

Circle each item on the right, which you remember from the Max's list (located on the previous page).

➡

chair	cabinet	bench
wallpaper	mat	cart
partition	tray	desk
sculpture	clock	stand
bookends	stool	tray
binders	box	rug
calendar	vase	basket

Solution on page 136

The Memory Challenge

This is a very challenging short-term memory game. Below is a list of seven unrelated words. The goal is to memorize the words, then turn the page, and write down the words in order.

The List:

1. Wall

2. Kangaroo

3. Yarn

4. Tile

5. Gum

6. Walk

7. Mail

8. Gift

A HINT... (or how to make this challenge doable)

To help memorize a list of unrelated items, you can use your imagination to make the items more memorable.

For example, if you were trying to remember the list:

> A. Horse
> B. Book
> C. Apple tree

You could imagine..... A horse (Item A) is trotting along. The horse spots a Book (Item B), and picks it up with its mouth. The horse carries the book to his favorite apple tree (Item C) to read the story.

Consider trying this approach with the list to the left.

Turn the page when you have memorized the items.

This puzzle continues from the previous page.

The Memory Challenge Continued

Write the eight items you memorized from the previous page in the spaces provided.

1. _____

2. _____

3. _____

4. _____

5. _____

6. _____

7. _____

8. _____

Brain Game

WELL MADE WORDS

Create words out of the letters provided. You can use each letter only once per word.

LETTERS

WORDS

T P

M R

S

O

_____   _____

_____   _____

_____   _____

_____   _____

_____   _____

_____   _____

_____   _____

Solution on page 137

- 28 -

Memory Activities, Puzzles, and Brain Games

Fashion and Accessories

Includes Delightful Details, Starts With, Silly Sentences, Cool Categories, Particular Pictures, Lovely Memories, Backwards, Word Search, Sudoku, Odd One Out, Well Made Words, and The Memory Challenge

Starts with "B"

In this memory puzzle, the answer to each clue begins with the letter "B" and relates to this section's theme of "Fashion & Accessories."

1. Delightful decoration that may adorn a person's wrist.

2. A container that is used by business people to carry their work.

3. A soft cap that is made of fabric and is often part of a uniform.

4. Item worn for lounging around the house or after a shower.

5. A piece of jewelery that is often attached to clothing with a pin.

6. Fabric accessory that dresses up a quality tuxedo.

7. High-end store that specializes in women's fashion.

8. Gem placed in jewelery that changes depending on when you're born.

Solution on page 137

PARTICULAR PICTURES

Take a look at the three pieces of jewelery below. Take your time to memorize the items. Next, turn the page and pick out the three items of jewelery that you memorized.

Turn the page to continue

This puzzle continues from the previous page.

PARTICULAR PICTURES..... CONTINUED

Did you study the three pieces of jewelery on the previous page? Great! Now circle the items that you memorized.

Silly Sentences...

Take some time to memorize the silly sentence below. Then pick it out from a selection of four similar sentences on the next page. Then repeat for the second silly sentence!

Sentence One:

"Joyce jumps for joy when she sees emerald earrings."

turn the page ➡

. . . .

Sentence Two:

"Trevor travels with a silk scarf and a wonky watch."

turn the page ➡

This puzzle continues from the previous page.

SILLY SENTENCES..... CONTINUED

Sentence One:

Pick the silly sentence you memorized on the previous page from the four options below.

A) Joyce jumps for joy when she sees emerald earrings.

B) Jen jumps for joy when she sees emerald earrings.

C) Joyce jumps for joy when she sees jade earrings.

D) Joyce jumps for joy when she sees jade jewelery.

....

Sentence Two:

Pick the silly sentence you memorized on the previous page from the four options below.

A) Trevor travels with a silk scarf and a wind up watch.

B) Trevor travels with a wool scarf and a wonky watch.

C) Trevor packed a silk scarf and a wonky watch.

D) Trevor travels with a silk scarf and a wonky watch.

Solution on page 137

Lovely Memories...

Describe your favorite outfit — whether it was wedding dress or a casual outfit. Try to recall interesting details including the color and texture of the fabrics, the accessories that you wore, and the shoes that went with the outfit.

_____
_____
_____
_____
_____
_____
_____
_____
_____
_____
_____
_____
_____
_____
_____
_____
_____
_____
_____
_____

Cool Categories!

Make a list of different kinds and styles of shoes. How many types of shoes can you think of?

1. _____
2. _____
3. _____
4. _____
5. _____
6. _____
7. _____
8. _____
9. _____
10. _____
11. _____
12. _____
13 _____
14. _____
15. _____
16. _____
17. _____
18. _____
19. _____
20. _____
21. _____

Make a list of all of the items you might find at a jewelry store. How many items can you think of?

1. _____
2. _____
3. _____
4. _____
5. _____
6. _____
7. _____
8. _____
9. _____
10. _____
11. _____
12. _____
13 _____
14. _____
15. _____
16. _____
17. _____
18. _____
19. _____
20. _____
21. _____

Solution on page 137

Delightful Details

1. Take a look at the blazer to the right. On the next page is an identical blazer, that is missing one detail. When you are ready, turn the page and fill in the missing detail.

Turn the page to continue ➤

2. Take a look at the earrings to the right. On the next page is an identical set of earrings, that is missing one detail. When you are ready, turn the page and fill in the missing detail.

Turn the page to continue ➤

These two puzzles continue from the previous page.

1. Have you studied the blazer on the previous page? Great! Now draw in the one detail that will make the blazer to the right, identical to the image on the previous page.

Draw in the 1 missing detail!

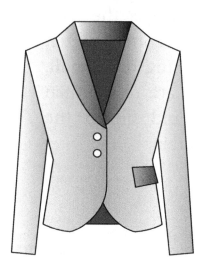

From the previous page

2. Have you studied the earrings on the previous page? Great! Now draw in the one detail that will make the earrings to the right, identical to the image on the previous page.

Draw in the 1 missing detail!

From the previous page

Solution on page 138

FIND THE 5 DIFFERENCES

Find the 5 differences between the two set of accessories.

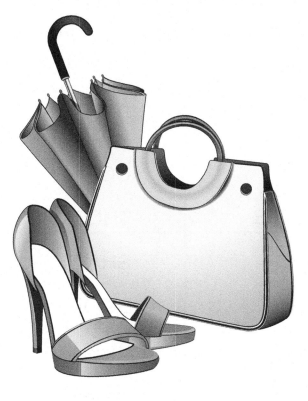

WORD SEARCH
WINTER FASHION

In this classic puzzle, the goal is to find all the words listed below, within the letter grid on the right. Each word is placed in a straight line; either horizontally, vertically or diagonally in the grid.

WORD LIST:

CORDS	GLOVES	COAT
QUILT	EARMUFFS	THERMAL
JUMPER	PONCHO	SHAWL
SLIPPERS	TWEED	BOOTS
CARDIGAN	JACKET	BEANIE
SWEATER	CASHMERE	WARM
PARKA	TURTLENECK	TIGHTS
VEST	FLANNEL	HOODIE
CLEATS	WOOL	PULLOVER
FLEECE	MITTENS	SCARF
DENIM	DOWN	LAYER

```
X  Q  L  P  A  T  U  R  T  L  E  N  E  C  K  Q  E
T  P  C  I  C  P  C  M  V  F  Y  V  D  Z  C  L  D
Z  J  A  K  P  W  D  Q  V  S  C  S  X  C  H  X  O
O  T  R  N  E  A  R  M  U  F  F  S  G  L  O  C  W
C  I  D  G  L  O  V  E  S  T  D  S  O  E  O  M  N
S  G  I  L  A  Y  E  R  P  U  V  T  L  A  D  P  T
H  H  G  T  W  E  E  D  C  U  C  E  O  T  I  A  G
A  T  A  C  W  J  Y  Z  O  G  L  U  S  S  E  R  D
W  S  N  Q  O  E  Y  C  A  C  P  L  Q  T  C  K  E
L  Z  Y  H  L  R  C  K  T  F  O  Z  O  U  I  A  N
S  W  O  O  L  L  D  K  H  P  N  F  P  V  U  T  I
J  F  V  L  W  N  B  S  K  Z  C  P  H  H  E  G  M
U  M  I  T  T  E  N  S  F  S  H  C  O  Q  S  R  X
M  L  F  L  A  N  N  E  L  S  O  B  V  U  S  F  A
P  V  H  R  V  G  N  X  P  E  J  O  G  I  C  D  L
E  A  M  S  L  I  P  P  E  R  S  O  F  L  A  W  F
R  Q  T  I  J  A  C  K  E  T  Z  T  L  T  R  S  V
B  I  F  B  V  N  F  W  A  R  M  S  E  S  F  X  N
A  U  C  B  A  Y  W  C  A  S  H  M  E  R  E  A  Y
K  W  R  X  S  W  E  A  T  E  R  M  C  L  S  C  L
Y  A  C  Z  T  H  E  R  M  A  L  G  E  Z  V  Z  E
B  E  A  N  I  E  O  U  P  D  X  Z  E  N  S  Z  J
```

Solution on page 138   - 41 -

BACKWARDS SDRAWKCAB

In this activity, the goal is to write out the sentence backwards. To increase the level of difficulty of this memory challenge, you can minimize the number of times you refer to the original sentence.

1.   Don't judge a book by its cover.

Write it
backwards: _____

2.   Better late then never.

Write it
backwards: _____

3.   Always put your best foot forward.

Write it
backwards: _____

4.   Wide will wear, but tight will tear.

Write it
backwards: _____

Solution on page 138

FUN WITH SUDOKU

In this brain game, the goal is to use the numbers 1 to 9 to fill in the grid below. In particular, there are three rules:

1. Each horizontal row needs to have the all of the numbers from 1 to 9, only once.
2. Each vertical row needs to have all the numbers from 1 to 9, only once.
3. Each 3 by 3 square has the numbers from 1 to 9, only once.

5	6	2	3		7	9	4	
	9	1		8	2	5	7	3
7		3	9	5	4		1	2
9		6	7	2		4		1
1	2	5	4		9	8		7
		7	5	3	1	2	9	
		9	2	4	6	1	8	5
2	5	8	1			7		4
6	1		8	7	5	3	2	

Solution on page 139   - 43 -

SPOT THE ODD ONE OUT

Find the hat that is different from the rest.

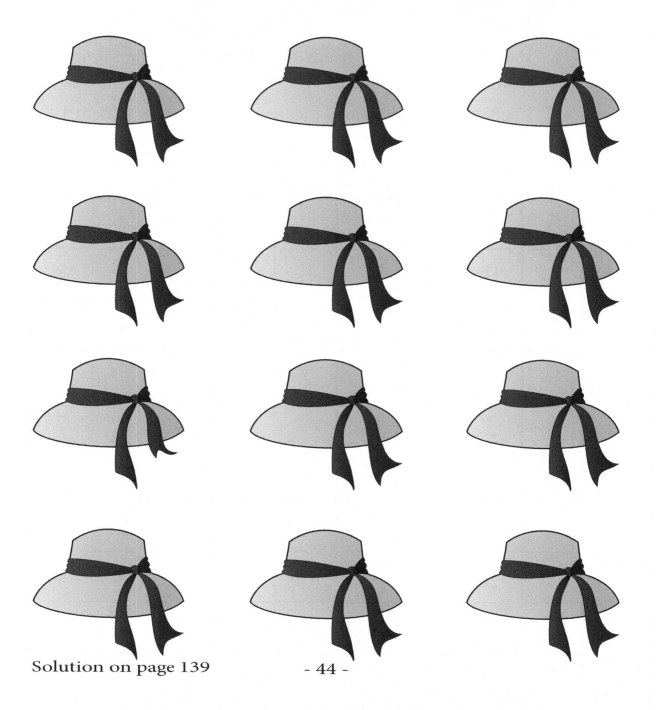

Solution on page 139

The Memory Challenge

This is a very challenging short-term memory game. Below is a list of seven unrelated words. The goal is to memorize the words, then turn the page, and write down the words in order.

The List:

1. Ring

2. Sidewalk

3. Cookie

4. Shoe

5. Snail

6. Purse

7. Tissue

8. Truck

A HINT... (or how to make this challenge doable)

To help memorize a list of unrelated items, you can use your imagination to make the items more memorable.

For example, if you were trying to remember the list:

  A. Horse
  B. Book
  C. Apple tree

You could imagine..... A horse (Item A) is trotting along. The horse spots a Book (Item B), and picks it up with its mouth. The horse carries the book to his favorite apple tree (Item C) to read the story.

Consider trying this approach with the list to the left.

Turn the page when you have memorized the items.

This puzzle is continues from the previous page.

The Memory Challenge Continued

Write the eight items you memorized from the previous page in the spaces provided.

1. _____

2. _____

3. _____

4. _____

5. _____

6. _____

7. _____

8. _____

Brain Game

WELL MADE WORDS

Create words out of the letters provided. You can use each letter only once per word.

LETTERS

A
K
L
W
R
E

WORDS

_____ _____

_____ _____

_____ _____

_____ _____

_____ _____

_____ _____

Solution on page 139

Memory Activities, Puzzles, and Brain Games

Arts and Crafts

Includes Starts With, Cool Categories, Particular Pictures, Lovely Memories, Terrific Lists, Well Made Words, Word Search, Sudoku, Find the Differences, Odd One Out Two of a Kind and The Memory Challenge

Starts with "P"

In this memory puzzle, the answer to each clue begins with the letter "P" and relates to this section's theme of "Arts & Crafts."

1. A popular art form that uses clay and extreme heat.

2. Used to mix and hold paint that will be used on a canvas.

3. A type of pigment and binder; or a soft color hue.

4. A drawing, painting or photograph of a particular person.

5. Collection of a person's artwork that represents their body of work.

6. A decorative or artistic design, that repeats itself.

7. An undercoat of paint that makes a surface ready to paint.

8. An image that is created by using a camera.

Solution on page 139

PARTICULAR PICTURES

Take a look at the three sewing items below. Take your time to memorize the items. Next, turn the page and pick out the three items that you memorized.

This puzzle continues from the previous page.

PARTICULAR PICTURES..... CONTINUED

Did you study the three sewing items on the previous page? Great! Now circle the three items that you memorized.

Solution on page 140   - 50 -

Silly Sentences...

Take some time to memorize the silly sentence below. Then pick it out from a selection of four similar sentences on the next page. Then repeat for the second silly sentence!

Sentence One:

"Crafty Karen is gluing glitter to Ken's card."

turn the page

• •

Sentence Two:

"Henry paints a portrait of his nice niece."

turn the page

This puzzle continues from the previous page.

SILLY SENTENCES..... CONTINUED

Sentence One:

Pick the silly sentence you memorized on the previous page from the four options below.

A) Crafty Kim is gluing stickers to Ken's card.

B) Crafty Kim is gluing sparkles to Ken's card.

C) Crafty Karen didn't glue glitter to Ken's card

D) Crafty Karen is gluing glitter to Ken's card.

....

Sentence Two:

Pick the silly sentence you memorized on the previous page from the four options below.

A) Henry paints a portrait of his nice niece.

B) Henry draws a portrait of his nice nephew.

C) Henry takes a photograph of his nice niece.

D) Harold paints a portrait of his new nephew.

Solution on page 140

Lovely Memories...

Take some time to write about your favorite craft project — whether it was putting together a scrapbook, a Halloween display or making a holiday card. Try to recall interesting details including the materials that you used and how you made the project.

_____

_____

_____

_____

_____

_____

_____

_____

_____

_____

_____

_____

_____

_____

_____

_____

_____

_____

_____

_____

Cool Categories!

Make a list of different kinds of fabric (such as silk). How many kinds of fabric can you think of?	Make a list of all of the items you might use when doing a woodworking project. How many can you think of?

1.	1.
2.	2.
3.	3.
4.	4.
5.	5.
6.	6.
7.	7.
8.	8.
9.	9.
10.	10.
11.	11.
12.	12.
13	13
14.	14.
15.	15.
16.	16.
17.	17.
18.	18.
19.	19.
20.	20.
21.	21.

Solution on page 140

SPOT THE ODD ONE OUT

Find the eraser that is different from the rest.

Solution on page 140

WORD SEARCH
CRAFT SUPPLIES

In this classic puzzle, the goal is to find all the words listed below, within the letter grid on the right. Each word is placed in a straight line; either horizontally, vertically or diagonally in the grid.

WORD LIST:

BRUSH	PEN	PAPER
THREAD	WIRE	FELT
TINSEL	PINS	GLAZE
JOURNAL	TAPE	FABRIC
BELLS	BEADS	CHALK
PENCIL	SCISSORS	PAINT
SEQUINS	RIBBON	TRIM
STICKERS	YARN	STYROFOAM
CUTTER	BUTTONS	GLUE
INK	PATTERN	TISSUE
CLAY	GLITTER	FEATHERS

```
R I B B O N W G G F C G L B T T Q
N A E S P E D E L R E T W C H R F
A W L T R G J V L U E L B L R I H
L J L U P B Y E S Y E E T A E M C
M O S B A U E P E N O W O Y A I N
Y U Z X I J W A W F P J V F D R W
N R Z W N P R U D T E Y G F P H I
G N M B T B T I E S N M Z E P I R
F A O F R H D N O U C W R A B M E
P L I D R U S K G Y I K U T U W X
C I R G H N S E Z H L N G H T W Z
B O N M L Y R H Q S L K B E T P G
M T H S M G T H Z U C W O R O A L
W E X P A T T E R N I I J S N P I
S T Y R O F O A M C U N S L S E T
L O K H G E Z M Y B U O S S M R T
F K J F R R C H A L K T D X O N E
V S Y A R N D E Q E N O T W V R R
F P W T I N S E L C Z X X E E S S
V S T I C K E R S E Q D D K R G U
T A P E C W L X R T G L A Z E N P
S Q T I S S U E I B F A B R I C K
```

FIND THE 5 DIFFERENCES

Find the 5 differences between the two photographers.

Solution on page 141

Terrific Lists... Redecoration

In these puzzles, the goal is to memorize the list of items; and then turn the page and circle the items you remember.

Brent is going shopping for his woodworking project. To the right is a list of items he wants to buy, so he can get started. Take some time to memorize his list, then turn the page.

Brent's List

board	dowel
pencil	filler
saw	shellac

turn the page

Laura is going shopping for her quilt project. To the right is a list of items she wants to buy so she can get started. Take some time to memorize Laura's list, then turn the page.

Laura's List

thread	ruler
iron	pins
mat	clips

turn the page

This puzzle continues from the previous page.

Brent's List

Circle each item on the right, which you remember from the Brent's list (located on the previous page).

nails	shellac	screws
vacuum	dowel	nails
hammer	chisel	plank
pencil	level	knife
filler	paint	glue
stickers	template	board
pliers	wire	saw

Laura's List

Circle each item on the right, which you remember from the Laura's list (located on the previous page).

batting	thread	tape
hoop	thimble	clips
iron	stencil	fabric
glue	pins	blade
cutter	buttons	beads
mat	scissors	lamp
tassels	fleece	ruler

Solution on page 141

FUN WITH SUDOKU

In this brain game, the goal is to use the numbers 1 to 9 to fill in the grid below. In particular, there are three rules:

1. Each horizontal row needs to have the all of the numbers from 1 to 9, only once.
2. Each vertical row needs to have all the numbers from 1 to 9, only once.
3. Each 3 by 3 square has the numbers from 1 to 9, only once.

1	3	2		7		8	4	9
	7	9	2	8	3		6	5
	5	8	1	9	4		2	3
8	1		3	6	2	4	9	7
2		6	7	1	9	3		8
7	9	3		4	5	2	1	6
	6	7	4	2	8	5	3	
5	2	1	9			6	8	
3	8		6	5	1		7	2

FIND TWO OF A KIND

Find the two scissors that are identical.

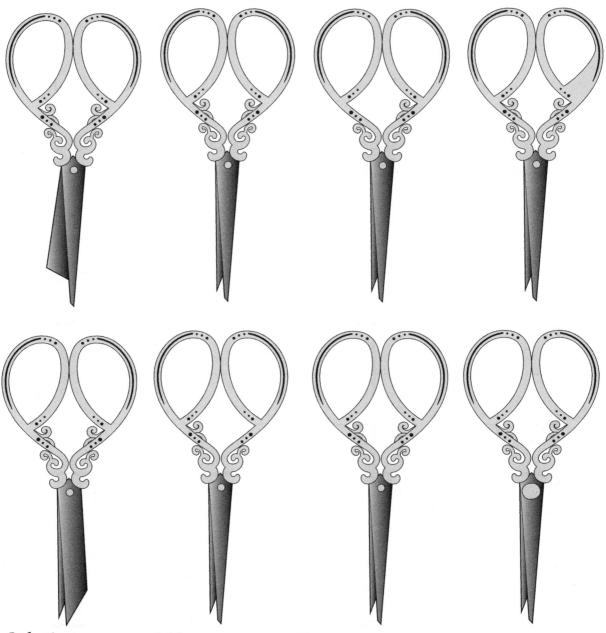

Solution on page 142   - 62 -

The Memory Challenge

This is a very challenging short-term memory game. Below is a list of seven unrelated words. The goal is to memorize the words, then turn the page, and write down the words in order.

The List:

1. Suit

2. Scarf

3. Milk

4. Mop

5. Paper

6. Scissors

7. Tape

8. Cup

A HINT... (or how to make this challenge doable)

To help memorize a list of unrelated items, you can use your imagination to make the items more memorable.

For example, if you were trying to remember the list:

> A. Horse
> B. Book
> C. Apple tree

You could imagine..... A horse (Item A) is trotting along. The horse spots a Book (Item B), and picks it up with its mouth. The horse carries the book to his favorite apple tree (Item C) to read the story.

Consider trying this approach with the list to the left.

Turn the page when you have memorized the items.

This puzzle continues from the previous page.

The Memory Challenge Continued

Write the eight words you memorized from the previous page in the spaces provided.

1. _____

2. _____

3. _____

4. _____

5. _____

6. _____

7. _____

8. _____

Brain Game

WELL MADE WORDS

Create words out of the letters provided. You can use each letter only once per word.

LETTERS

G
I
L
N
P
A

WORDS

_____   _____

_____   _____

_____   _____

_____   _____

_____   _____

_____   _____

Solution on page 142

Memory Activities, Puzzles, and Brain Games

Our Beautiful Earth

Includes Delightful Details, Starts With, Cool Categories, Silly Sentences, Particular Pictures, Lovely Memories, Merry Matching, Word Search, Sudoku, Two of a Kind, Odd One Out and The Memory Challenge

Starts with "G"

In this memory puzzle, the answer to each clue begins with the letter "G" and relates to this section's theme of "Our Beautiful Earth."

1. An huge body of dense ice that slowly moves because of its weight.

_____

2. A satellite-based navigation system that can guide users.

_____

3. A dominant color in nature, mixture of blue and yellow.

_____

4. The science of studying the earth and its many features.

_____

5. Type of igneous rock, often used for kitchen counter tops.

_____

6. Law of nature that causes an apple to fall to the earth.

_____

7. Type of large brown bear that is found in parts of North America.

_____

8. A large inlet of ocean water partially surrounded by land.

_____

Solution on page 142

Delightful Details

Take a look at the flower below. On the next page is an identical picture, that is missing two details. When you are ready, turn the page and fill in the missing details.

This puzzle continues from the previous page.

Delightful Details... continued

Have you studied the flower on the previous page? Great! Now draw in the two details that will make the flower below identical to the image on the previous page.

Draw in the 2 missing details!

Solution on page 142

Silly Sentences...

Memorize the silly sentence below. Then see if you can pick it out from a selection of four similar sentences on the next page. Then repeat for the second silly sentence!

Sentence One:

"The lovely lake is full of feisty fish."

turn the page ➡

. . . .

Sentence Two:

"In the fabulous forest, birds sing super songs."

turn the page ➡

This puzzle continues from the previous page.

SILLY SENTENCES..... CONTINUED

Sentence One:

Pick the silly sentence you memorized on the previous page from the four options below.

A) The beautiful lake is full of feisty fish.

B) The lovely lake is full of feisty fish.

C) The lovely lake is full of friendly fish.

D) The lovely lake is missing feisty fish.

....

Sentence Two:

Pick the silly sentence you memorized on the previous page from the four options below.

A) In the fabulous jungle, birds sing super songs.

B) In the fabulous forest, birds hum super songs.

C) In the fabulous forest, birds sing super songs.

D) In the fabulous forest, people sing super songs.

Solution on page 143

PARTICULAR PICTURES

Take a look at the three nature icons below. Take your time to memorize them. Next, turn the page and pick out the three nature items that you memorized.

Turn the page to continue

This puzzle continues from the previous page.

PARTICULAR PICTURES..... CONTINUED

Did you study the three nature items on the previous page? Great!
Now circle the three items that you memorized.

Solution on page 143

Lovely Memories...

Take some time to write about your favorite body of water — whether its a river you fished in, or a lake you visited when your were younger, or an ocean on whose beach you relaxed during a vacation. Consider what the water and surrounding area looked like. What did you do at the water's edge or in the water?

_____

_____

_____

_____

_____

_____

_____

_____

_____

_____

_____

_____

_____

_____

_____

_____

_____

_____

_____

_____

_____

FIND TWO OF A KIND

Find the two trees that are identical.

Solution on page 143

Cool Categories!

Make a list of the names of large bodies of water. How many different ones can you think of?

1. _____
2. _____
3. _____
4. _____
5. _____
6. _____
7. _____
8. _____
9. _____
10. _____
11. _____
12. _____
13 _____
14. _____
15. _____
16. _____
17. _____
18. _____
19. _____
20. _____
21. _____

Make a list of different kinds of rocks or gemstones. How many rocks or gemstones can you think of?

1. _____
2. _____
3. _____
4. _____
5. _____
6. _____
7. _____
8. _____
9. _____
10. _____
11. _____
12. _____
13 _____
14. _____
15. _____
16. _____
17. _____
18. _____
19. _____
20. _____
21. _____

Solution on page 143

WORD SEARCH

STORMY WEATHER

In this classic puzzle, the goal is to find all the words listed below, within the letter grid on the right. Each word is placed in a straight line; either horizontally, vertically or diagonally in the grid.

WORD LIST:

SLEET	HAIL	TYPHOON
GALE	DOWNPOUR	TWISTER
CYCLONE	FORECAST	BLEAK
HEAT	GUST	FREEZE
SNOW	TSUNAMI	SANDSTORM
FOG	HUMID	HURRICANE
FLOOD	TORNADO	LANDFALL
FRIGID	MONSOON	WINDY
DARK	RAIN	CHILL
VORTEX	THUNDER	LIGHTNING
BLIZZARD	ELEMENT	RIPTIDE

```
D W G A L E L F T R J H O I Y C F
C W U N A F B K I H C K R A I N L
F R E E Z E H U R R I C A N E Q O
T V O R T E X N N H U M I D A O O
C H P Q A D O W N P O U R I H C D
W B D O L A R T B L I Z Z A R D F
L N L A F O R E C A S T S M Z I J
Z R J E R F S L L D T F F O L Y L
T U P A A K L T A N N O F N D J O
O Z V U I K E Z H N R G M S Q S B
R C H I L L E F T U D B P O P T L
N T P B X U T R M V N F T O D S U
A V K W I N D Y Z J U D A N T U S
D G P P E L E M E N T Q E L N N T
O A L I G H T N I N G B O R L A E
H C F T W I S T E R U W U D R M R
A D G B Z T Y P H O O N O F T I H
I V U S N Q H I G U C Y C L O N E
L E S N X A E O H D E Q K N X C P
M S T O H I A I H N A F R I G I D
K N B W S J T T S A N D S T O R M
T J T L J E S Z R I P T I D E O H
```

MERRY MATCHING

How many times can you find this sequence of icons in a straight line in the grid below?

NOTE: The sequence of icons can be located vertically, diagonally, or horizontally in the gird. Also, the sequence of icons may be found forwards or backwards.

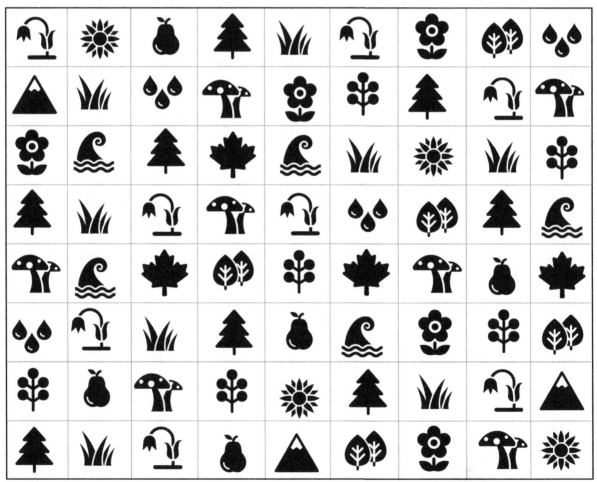

Solution on page 144

Terrific Lists... Time Outdoors

In these puzzles, the goal is to memorize the list of items; and then turn the page and circle the items you remember.

George is going camping on the weekend. To the right is a list of items he wants to buy, so he is ready for his trip. Once you think you've memorized his list turn the page.

George's List

cooler	tent
tote	blanket
thermos	paddle

turn the page

Wendy is going mountain climbing. To the right is a list of items she wants to buy so she can get started. Once you think you've memorized her list turn the page.

Wendy's List

boots	rope
poles	pulley
anchor	picket

turn the page

This puzzle continues from the previous page.

George's List

Circle any item on the right, which you remember from the George's list (located on the previous page)

light	matches	filter
cooler	tarp	tote
mat	thermos	watch
stove	grill	lock
blanket	knife	spoon
plate	soap	tent
towel	paddle	t-shirt

Wendy's List

Circle any item on the right, which you remember from the Wendy's list (located on the previous page)

boots	cable	poles
hook	shovel	hat
pulley	helmet	picket
purifier	map	GPS
radio	anchor	axe
whistle	gloves	socks
crampons	rope	cords

Solution on page 144

FUN WITH SUDOKU

In this brain game, the goal is to use the numbers 1 to 9 to fill in the grid below. In particular, there are three rules:

1. Each horizontal row needs to have the all of the numbers from 1 to 9, only once.

2. Each vertical row needs to have all the numbers from 1 to 9, only once.

3. Each 3 by 3 square has the numbers from 1 to 9, only once.

7	3			2	8	6	4	1
	2	6	4	1	3	5		9
5		4	6			8	2	
	9	2	7	3	1		5	8
	7	5	8		4	9		2
4	8	3		5	9	1	6	7
2	4	1	3	8			9	5
9			1	4	2	3	8	6
3	6	8		7	5	2	1	

Solution on page 145

SPOT THE ODD ONE OUT

Find the picture that is different from the rest.

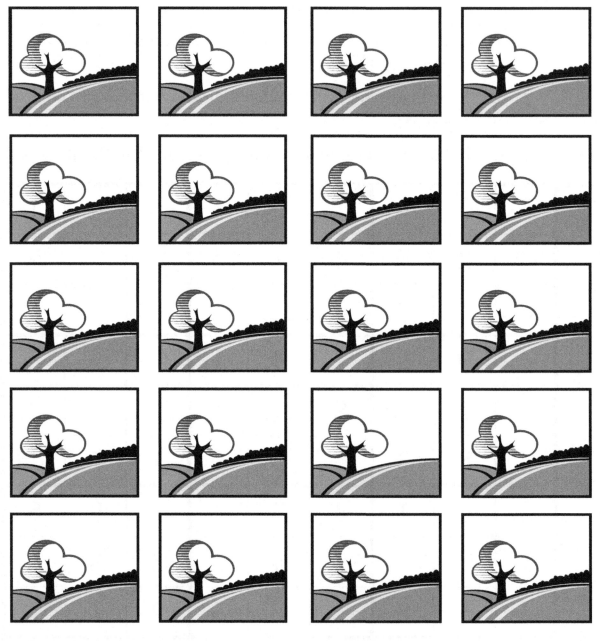

Solution on page 145

The Memory Challenge

This is a very challenging short-term memory game. Below is a list of seven unrelated words. The goal is to memorize the words, then turn the page, and write down the words in order.

The List:

1. **Beaver**

2. **Ice Cream**

3. **Lake**

4. **Spoon**

5. **Grass**

6. **Pen**

7. **Field**

8. **Hole**

A HINT... (or how to make this challenge doable)

To help memorize a list of unrelated items, you can use your imagination to make the items more memorable.

For example, if you were trying to remember the list:

> A. Horse
> B. Book
> C. Apple tree

You could imagine..... A horse (Item A) is trotting along. The horse spots a Book (Item B), and picks it up with its mouth. The horse carries the book to his favorite apple tree (Item C) to read the story.

Consider trying this approach with the list to the left.

Turn the page when you have memorized the items.

Solution on page 145

This puzzle continues from the previous page.

The Memory Challenge Continued

Write the eight items you memorized from the previous page in the spaces provided.

1. _____

2. _____

3. _____

4. _____

5. _____

6. _____

7. _____

8. _____

Brain Game

WELL MADE WORDS

Create words out of the letters provided. You can use each letter only once per word.

LETTERS

E
R
O
A
D
F

WORDS

_____ _____

_____ _____

_____ _____

_____ _____

_____ _____

_____ _____

Solution on page 145

Memory Activities, Puzzles, and Brain Games

Love of Animals

Includes Delightful Details, Starts With, Cool Categories, Silly Sentences, Particular Pictures, Lovely Memories, Word Search, Terrific Lists, Two of a Kind, Well Made Words and The Memory Challenge

Starts with "C"

In this memory puzzle, the answer to each clue begins with the letter "C" and relates to this section's theme of "Love of Animals."

1. Animal that does well in the desert and has a hump on its back.

_____

2. A large bird that has both long legs and a long neck.

_____

3. A big aquatic reptile with thick skin, long jaws and sharp teeth.

_____

4. A wild canine that is known for its howl and living in packs.

_____

5. An adult female bovine, often raised to provide milk.

_____

6. A strong wild cat that is also known as a mountain lion.

_____

7. It has pincers, an exoskeleton and may walk sideways.

_____

8. Native to Africa, it is a species of great ape with long arms.

_____

Solution on page 145

PARTICULAR PICTURES

Take a look at the three animals below. Take your time to memorize the animals. Then turn the page and pick out the three animals that you memorized.

Turn the page to continue

This puzzle continues from the previous page.

PARTICULAR PICTURES..... CONTINUED

Did you study the three animals on the previous page? Great! Now circle the three items that you memorized.

Silly Sentences...

Take some time to memorize the silly sentence below. Then pick it out from a selection of four similar sentences on the next page. Then repeat for the second silly sentence!

Sentence One:

"The delightful dog likes to eat peanut butter."

turn the page ⟶

Sentence Two:

"The wonderful walrus rests on the extra, cold ice."

turn the page ⟶

SILLY SENTENCES..... CONTINUED

Sentence One:

Pick the silly sentence you memorized on the previous page from the four options below.

A) The delightful dog likes to eat peanut butter.

B) The delightful dog likes to eat apple butter.

C) The determined dog likes to eat peanut butter.

D) The delightful dog likes to eat treats.

. . . .

Sentence Two:

Pick the silly sentence you memorized on the previous page from the four options below.

A) The wonderful seal rests on the extra, cold ice.

B) The wonderful seal walks on the extra, cold ice.

C) The wonderful walrus rests on the extra, cold ice.

D) The sleepy walrus rests on the extra, cold ice.

Solution on page 146   - 90 -

Lovely Memories...

Take some time to write about your favorite type of wild animal — have you ever seen the animal in real life? When? Describe the features of the animal in some detail. In your opinion, what makes this kind of animal interesting and unique?

_____

_____

_____

_____

_____

_____

_____

_____

_____

_____

_____

_____

_____

_____

_____

_____

_____

_____

_____

Cool Categories!

Make a list of different kinds of birds. How many different species can you think of?

1. _____
2. _____
3. _____
4. _____
5. _____
6. _____
7. _____
8. _____
9. _____
10. _____
11. _____
12. _____
13 _____
14. _____
15. _____
16. _____
17. _____
18. _____
19. _____
20. _____
21. _____

Make a list of different kinds of animals that have fur. How many different species can you think of?

1. _____
2. _____
3. _____
4. _____
5. _____
6. _____
7. _____
8. _____
9. _____
10. _____
11. _____
12. _____
13 _____
14. _____
15. _____
16. _____
17. _____
18. _____
19. _____
20. _____
21. _____

Solution on page 146

FIND THE 5 DIFFERENCES

Find the 5 differences between the dog groomers.

WORD SEARCH
BEAUTIFUL BEARS

In this classic puzzle, the goal is to find all the words listed below, within the letter grid on the right. Each word is placed in a straight line; either horizontally, vertically or diagonally in the grid.

WORD LIST:

LARGE	MAMMAL	SOLITARY
SHAGGY	SWIM	CAVE
YOGI	POWERFUL	CUB
BLACK	SLOTH	PAWS
HIBERNATE	FOREST	STAND
TAIL	GRIZZLY	HONEY
KODIAK	STRONG	HUNT
OMNIVORE	ROAM	ATTACK
POLAR	BROWN	ENDANGERED
WHITE	PANDA	CLIMB
DEN	SNOUT	FUR

```
S  P  B  R  O  W  N  L  P  O  N  H  F  O  D  P  M
M  H  U  F  V  S  T  L  A  R  O  A  M  Y  E  O  I
B  H  K  G  L  H  K  N  E  C  M  S  P  V  N  L  B
A  S  J  O  L  A  K  K  Z  N  N  R  F  A  T  A  A
Y  S  T  D  D  T  R  P  W  Z  I  G  J  P  W  R  M
F  C  W  R  H  I  Y  G  P  R  V  N  S  D  C  S  X
B  F  U  I  O  O  A  O  E  S  O  A  H  F  F  D  C
T  R  Z  B  M  N  N  K  G  B  R  T  A  T  P  N  A
Z  B  D  F  U  R  G  E  D  I  E  H  G  K  B  G  V
M  V  G  U  X  N  X  C  Y  Z  W  L  G  Y  H  L  E
A  T  Q  N  S  L  O  T  H  U  K  Y  Y  D  I  J  H
M  O  S  N  O  U  T  C  L  W  H  I  T  E  B  H  W
M  D  U  R  X  P  O  W  E  R  F  U  L  M  E  E  V
A  E  N  D  A  N  G  E  R  E  D  P  X  A  R  D  F
L  S  G  P  I  H  U  N  T  O  O  B  V  I  N  S  C
O  T  W  A  D  Y  C  Z  B  S  O  L  I  T  A  R  Y
E  Z  I  N  K  I  P  A  Q  H  B  R  K  Q  T  M  N
H  V  P  D  T  A  I  L  F  M  K  L  D  I  E  P  L
C  H  P  A  D  G  R  I  Z  Z  L  Y  A  V  M  J  K
S  T  A  N  D  J  H  C  L  I  M  B  O  C  T  W  L
H  A  T  T  A  C  K  H  G  Z  Q  L  G  V  K  U  O
I  U  Y  W  K  L  T  I  U  B  J  F  O  R  E  S  T
```

FIND TWO OF A KIND

Find the two parrots that are identical.

Solution on page 147

Terrific Lists... Caring For Pets

In these puzzles, the goal is to memorize the list of items; and then turn the page and circle the items you remember.

June is going shopping to prepare for the arrival of her rescue dog Rufus. To the right is a list of items she wants to buy. Once you think you've memorized her list turn the page.

June's List

ball	towel
collar	leash
clippers	shampoo

turn the page

Liam is going to the pet store for his cat, Cookie. To the right is a list of items he wants to buy for Cookie. Once you think you've memorized Liam's list turn the page.

Liam's List

catnip	carrier
scratcher	litter
lounger	gate

turn the page

This puzzle continues from the previous page.

June's List

Circle any item on the right, which you remember from the June's list (located on the previous page).

bed	gates	rawhide
shampoo	brush	leash
ramp	ball	tag
pillow	toy	collar
baggies	coat	wipes
clippers	bowl	comb
towel	file	pads

Liam's List

Circle any item on the right, which you remember from the Liam's list (located on the previous page).

playpen	harness	carrier
cat door	feeder	scooper
gate	wipes	litter
scratcher	roller	sponge
wet food	post	catnip
spray	cover	bells
dry food	lounger	grass

Solution on page 147

Delightful Details

1. Take a look at the picture of the seal to the right. On the next page is an almost identical seal, that is missing one detail. When you are ready, turn the page and fill in the missing detail.

Turn the page to continue

2. Take a look at the mouse to the right. On the next page is an almost identical picture of a mouse, that is missing one detail. When you are ready, turn the page and fill in the missing detail.

Turn the page to continue

1. Have you studied the picture of the seal on the previous page? Terrific! Now draw in the one detail that will make the seal to the right, identical to the seal on the previous page.

From the previous page

Draw in the 1 missing detail!

2. Have you studied the picture of the mouse on the previous page? Super! Now draw in the one detail that will make the mouse to the right, identical to the mouse on the previous page.

From the previous page

Draw in the 1 missing detail!

Solution on page 147

The Memory Challenge

This is a very challenging short-term memory game. Below is a list of seven unrelated words. The goal is to memorize the words, then turn the page, and write down the words in order.

The List:

1. Goldfish

2. Key

3. Desk

4. Dog

5. Dinosaur

6. Rose

7. Water

8. Duck

A HINT... (or how to make this challenge doable)

To help memorize a list of unrelated items, you can use your imagination to make the items more memorable.

For example, if you were trying to remember the list:

> A. Horse
> B. Book
> C. Apple tree

You could imagine..... A horse (Item A) is trotting along. The horse spots a Book (Item B), and picks it up with its mouth. The horse carries the book to his favorite apple tree (Item C) to read the story.

Consider trying this approach with the list to the left.

Turn the page when you have memorized the items.

This puzzle continues from the previous page.

The Memory Challenge Continued

Write the eight items you memorized from the previous page in the spaces provided.

1. _____

2. _____

3. _____

4. _____

5. _____

6. _____

7. _____

8. _____

Brain Game

WELL MADE WORDS

Create words out of the letters provided. You can use each letter only once per word.

LETTERS

T
Y
L
P
E
A

WORDS

_____   _____

_____   _____

_____   _____

_____   _____

_____   _____

_____   _____

_____   _____

Solution on page 148

Memory Activities, Puzzles, and Brain Games

Making Music

Includes Starts With, Cool Categories, Particular Pictures, Lovely Memories, Silly Sentences, Word Search, Sudoku, Find the Differences, Lucky Lottery, Backwards, Odd One Out and The Memory Challenge

Starts with "T"

In this memory puzzle, the answer to each clue begins with the letter "T" and relates to this section's theme of "Making Music."

1. A simple melody that is often easy to remember.

_____

2. A brass instrument that has three valves and oblong-shaped tubing.

_____

3. The speed or rhythm that music should be played.

_____

4. Male singing voice that is higher than the baritone range.

_____

5. Trip often taken by bands, musicians or orchestras.

_____

6. Percussion instrument that has jingling metal disks.

_____

7. The quality of a musical note, also known as tone quality.

_____

8. Musical instrument with three sides, which is struck with a small rod.

_____

Solution on page 148

PARTICULAR PICTURES

Take a look at the three pictures of musical items below. Take your time to memorize the instruments. Then turn the page and pick out the three items that you memorized.

This puzzle continues from the previous page.

PARTICULAR PICTURES..... CONTINUED

Did you study the three instruments on the previous page? Great! Now circle the instruments that you memorized.

Solution on page 148

Silly Sentences...

Take some time to memorize the silly sentence below. Then pick it out from a selection of four similar sentences on the next page. Then repeat for the second silly sentence!

Sentence One:

"Patty plays the piccolo for a classical concert."

turn the page ➔

Sentence Two:

"David's drumming keepings his rock band humming."

turn the page ➔

This puzzle continues from the previous page.

SILLY SENTENCES..... CONTINUED

Sentence One:

Pick the silly sentence you memorized on the previous page from the four options below.

A) Max plays the piccolo for a classical concert.

B) Patty plays the piccolo for a rock concert.

C) Patty plays the flute for a classical concert.

D) Patty plays the piccolo for a classical concert.

....

Sentence Two:

Pick the silly sentence you memorized on the previous page from the four options below.

A) Trevor's drumming keeps his rock band humming.

B) David's drumming keeps his punk band humming.

C) David's drumming keeps his rock band humming.

D) David's playing keeps his rock band humming.

Solution on page 148

FIND THE 5 DIFFERENCES

Find the 5 differences between the two musicians.

WORD SEARCH
PLAYING PIANO

In this classic puzzle, the goal is to find all the words listed below, within the letter grid on the right. Each word is placed in a straight line; either horizontally, vertically or diagonally in the grid.

WORD LIST:

IVORIES	PEDAL	CADENCE
ADAGIO	SONATA	PERFORM
SCORE	TECHNIQUE	NOTES
TREBLE	SHARP	SCALE
KEYS	CONCERTO	MAJOR
PRACTICE	UPRIGHT	STRINGS
GRAND	FLAT	CHORD
LIBERACE	MELODY	CLEF
TIMBRE	MINOR	PITCH
TUNE	HAYDEN	STACCATO
MOZART	BEETHOVEN	CHOPIN

```
W  W  M  E  L  O  D  Y  N  V  A  L  C  E  K  R  R
V  D  T  C  S  O  S  U  M  P  S  D  P  L  E  M  R  R
C  B  Q  Z  P  F  Y  H  M  A  E  C  A  I  E  P  E
H  G  U  N  E  R  M  Z  A  O  O  R  A  G  T  F  N
A  T  F  D  B  X  A  I  T  R  P  K  F  L  I  C  P
Y  N  O  T  E  S  H  C  N  U  P  E  Y  O  E  O  H
D  V  O  C  H  O  R  D  T  O  J  Y  Z  N  R  L  U
E  W  I  V  O  R  I  E  S  I  R  S  N  X  A  M  U
N  P  E  D  A  L  D  T  H  J  C  G  M  F  Y  E  H
B  C  H  O  P  I  N  Y  E  K  R  E  A  M  S  E  G
M  J  A  T  E  C  H  N  I  Q  U  E  J  U  T  C  W
F  U  P  R  I  G  H  T  Y  M  A  R  O  R  A  O  E
S  X  H  H  C  Q  X  D  O  N  D  D  R  D  C  N  U
O  Q  I  H  T  L  I  S  C  O  R  E  N  B  C  C  D
N  F  Z  K  U  L  T  I  M  B  R  E  P  N  A  E  U
A  E  D  Z  U  S  M  O  Z  A  R  T  Q  C  T  R  G
T  E  T  U  N  E  L  I  B  E  R  A  C  E  O  T  H
A  M  S  T  R  I  N  G  S  A  K  U  A  M  B  O  F
S  V  O  L  U  K  P  B  E  E  T  H  O  V  E  N  L
L  H  I  O  K  N  G  R  A  N  D  G  G  L  P  B  A
V  O  S  Y  V  C  A  D  E  N  C  E  L  Y  B  X  T
S  I  X  K  K  V  L  R  N  T  R  E  B  L  E  O  U
```

FUN WITH SUDOKU

In this brain game, the goal is to use the numbers 1 to 9 to fill in the grid below. In particular, there are three rules:

1. Each horizontal row needs to have the all of the numbers from 1 to 9, only once.

2. Each vertical row needs to have all the numbers from 1 to 9, only once.

3. Each 3 by 3 square has the numbers from 1 to 9, only once.

	7	9		6	4	8		5
	4	8	5		7	3	2	9
2	1		9	8	3		7	4
8	2	3	4	9		7	6	
9			1	2	6	4		3
1	6	4	7		8	5	9	2
7	3	2	6		9		4	
	8		3	7	2	9	5	6
5	9		8	4		2	3	7

Solution on page 149   - 112 -

Lucky Lottery... Free Tickets

Take some time to memorize Ted's favorite numbers which he will use in a lottery for free concert tickets! Then turn the page and circle the numbers you remember in the number grid.

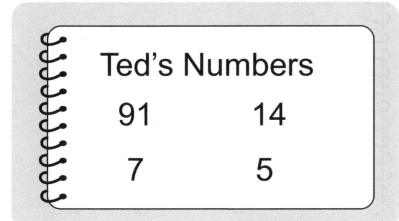

Ted's Numbers

91	14
7	5

Take some time to memorize Sara's favorite numbers which she will use in a lottery for free opera tickets! Then turn the page and circle the numbers you remember in the number grid.

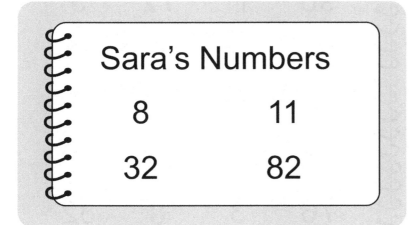

Sara's Numbers

8	11
32	82

This puzzle continues from the previous page.

Ted's Numbers

Have you looked at Ted's number list from the previous page? Now try to circle each number you remember in the number grid.

8	71	4	23
10	91	6	5
62	9	11	13
7	34	82	93
46	42	14	0
1	21	73	2

Sara's Numbers

Have you looked at Sara's number list from the previous page? Now try to circle each number you remember in the number grid.

32	5	92	7
96	11	72	3
81	24	5	71
9	74	62	6
64	23	17	19
76	3	8	82

Solution on page 149

SPOT THE ODD ONE OUT

Find the picture of the headphones from the rest.

Solution on page 149

Complete It!
Famous Musicals

In this memory game, the goal is to fill in the missing word in each popular musical.

1. *My _____ Lady*

2. *The _____ of the Opera*

3. *Beauty and the _____*

4. *Bye, ____ Birdie*

5. *How to Succeed in _____ With Really Trying*

6. *The Book of _____*

7. *Fiddle on the _____*

8. *A Funny Thing _____ on the Way to the Forum*

9. *The _____ of Music*

10. *Joseph and the _____ Technicolor Dreamcoat*

Solution on page 150   - 116 -

BACKWARDS SDRAWKCAB

In this activity, the goal is to write out the sentence backwards. Try to minimize the number of times you look at the original sentence to increase the level of difficulty of this memory challenge.

1. That's music to my ears!

Write it
backwards: _____

2. The concert is going to be wonderful.

Write it
backwards: _____

3. My favorite instrument is the saxophone.

Write it
backwards: _____

4. What a lovely melody!

Write it
backwards: _____

Solution on page 150

Cool Categories!

Make a list of different band or musical groups. How many different groups can you name?	Make a list of different famous solo singers. How many different singers can you name?

Make a list of different band or musical groups. How many different groups can you name?

1. _____
2. _____
3. _____
4. _____
5. _____
6. _____
7. _____
8. _____
9. _____
10. _____
11. _____
12. _____
13 _____
14. _____
15. _____
16. _____
17. _____
18. _____
19. _____
20. _____
21. _____

Make a list of different famous solo singers. How many different singers can you name?

1. _____
2. _____
3. _____
4. _____
5. _____
6. _____
7. _____
8. _____
9. _____
10. _____
11. _____
12. _____
13 _____
14. _____
15. _____
16. _____
17. _____
18. _____
19. _____
20. _____
21. _____

Solution on page 150

The Memory Challenge

This is a very challenging short-term memory game. Below is a list of seven unrelated words. The goal is to memorize the words, then turn the page, and write down the words in order.

The List:

1. Flute

2. Rabbit

3. Bubble

4. Pear

5. Guitar

6. Chair

7. Sidewalk

8. Sandwich

A HINT... (or how to make this challenge doable)

To help memorize a list of unrelated items, you can use your imagination to make the items more memorable.

For example, if you were trying to remember the list:

> A. Horse
> B. Book
> C. Apple tree

You could imagine..... A horse (Item A) is trotting along. The horse spots a Book (Item B), and picks it up with its mouth. The horse carries the book to his favorite apple tree (Item C) to read the story.

Consider trying this approach with the list to the left.

Turn the page when you have memorized the items.

This puzzle is continued from the previous page.

The Memory Challenge Continued

Write the eight items you memorized from the previous page in the spaces provided.

1. _____

2. _____

3. _____

4. _____

5. _____

6. _____

7. _____

8. _____

Brain Game

WELL MADE WORDS

Create words out of the letters provided. You can use each letter only once per word.

LETTERS

H
D
S
A
E I

WORDS

_____   _____

_____   _____

_____   _____

_____   _____

_____   _____

_____   _____

_____   _____

Solution on page 150

Memory Activities, Puzzles, and Brain Games

BONUS

Includes Word Search, Sudoku, Two of a Kind, Find the Differences, Unscramble, Spot the Odd One Out, Delightful Details, Shadow Finder and Lovely Memories

WORD SEARCH
TERRIFIC TREES

In this classic puzzle, the goal is to find all the words listed below, within the letter grid on the right. Each word is placed in a straight line; either horizontally, vertically or diagonally in the grid.

WORD LIST:

SHADE	BRANCH	FOREST
PINE	TRUNK	TIMBER
SPRUCE	WALNUT	WILLOW
JUNIPER	TOPIARY	BONSAI
ASPEN	EVERGREEN	ELM
SEEDS	MAPLE	CHESTNUT
MULBERRY	LEAF	DECIDUOUS
BEECH	LINDEN	BARK
BIRCH	PALM	CANOPY
OAK	SAP	CEDAR
FRUIT	ROOTS	REDWOOD

```
H C A K S A V V L T I M B E R H H
E N P B A J T P B R O B O N S A I
M N I I P O S W R R X P W W O C O
S Z V A G G S A J E O I P F N A
J U N I P E R P N Y V A P A O U K
A Y B W T I G R C S E W R U R V L
S R D V S N S U H T R R G W E Y E
B X O E K S Q C B R G J W A S K A
A V K O C D P E B C R I R L T N F
R D C O T I B B G S E D M N S F S
K D C M D S D O I V E D C U X Y E
M F T P E M W U S R N F A T L S L
T Z R A J P I T O C C A Q R Z J M
L H U L K M L F T U H H O X K X A
Q V N M E O L R T F S E N V H H R
G N K J I Q O U A O C H S E E D S
L B E E C H W I T G P C A T D X O
W Z F Y T X G T Y J R Q J D N J V
B C A N O P Y W I M A P L E E U Q
Z T E B P K R E D W O O D L B L T
V U J L I N D E N M U L B E R R Y
F E Q N I H B B E A S P E N T O O
```

FIND THE 5 DIFFERENCES

Find the 5 differences between the two men.

Solution on page 151

UNSCRAMBLE

RESTAURANT

In this brain teaser, the goal is to create words from the scrambled letters that are items related to a restaurant. The solution uses every letter provided to make the word. Place one letter into each square.

1. UMNE →

2. IWATRE →

3. SESDRTE →

4. FEHC →

5. BLAET →

6. FEFUBT →

7. NNDGII →

FUN WITH SUDOKU

In this brain game, the goal is to use the numbers 1 to 9 to fill in the grid below. In particular, there are three rules:

1. Each horizontal row needs to have the all of the numbers from 1 to 9, only once.

2. Each vertical row needs to have all the numbers from 1 to 9, only once.

3. Each 3 by 3 square has the numbers from 1 to 9, only once.

8	1	2			9	7	3	4
	5	9	4	3	1	2		8
6	3		2	8	7	1	9	
	6		9		2	8	4	7
4	9	5	6	7	8			2
		7	3	1		6	5	9
5	4	1		2	6	9		3
3			8	9	5	4		
9	7	8	1			5	2	6

Solution on page 151

FIND TWO OF A KIND

Find the two dogs that are identical.

Solution on page 151

SPOT THE ODD ONE OUT

Find the cookie that is different from the rest.

Solution on page 152   - 128 -

Delightful Details

Take a look at the picture of the lady playing cards below. On the next page is an identical picture, that is missing two details. When you are ready, turn the page and fill in the missing details.

This puzzle is continued from the previous page.

Delightful Details... continued

Have you studied the picture of the lady playing cards on the previous page? Terrific! Now draw in the two details that will make the image below identical to the picture on the previous page.

SHADOW FINDER

FIND THE PERFECT SHADOW FOR THE FOX

Solution on page 152

Lovely Memories...

Take some time to write about your favorite book— were to introduced to the book as an adult, or when you were a child? Describe the story. In your opinion, what makes your favorite book such a great read?

_____

_____

_____

_____

_____

_____

_____

_____

_____

_____

_____

_____

_____

_____

_____

_____

_____

_____

_____

ANSWERS

Page 8: Starts 'S'

1. Sofa
2. Shovel
3. Sink
4. Suitcase
5. Stairs
6. Shelf
7. Shower
8. Stool

Pages 9-10: Particular Pictures

Pages 11-12: Silly Sentences

Sentence One:
B) Larry loves to relax in his living room.

Sentence Two:
D) Sarah sips her tea while singing a song.

Pages 13-14: Details

Page 15: Find Differences

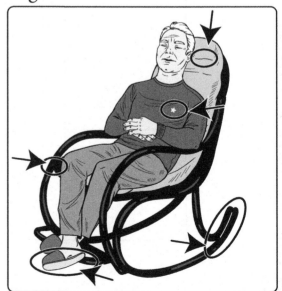

Answers

Pages 16-17: Word Search, Attic

Page 18: Odd One Out

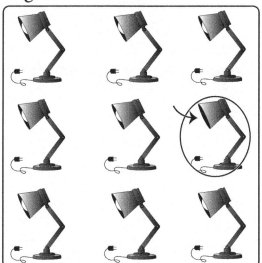

Page 19: Categories

Wall Items:

Shelf, mirror, nail, paint, light switch, photograph, television, art, wallpaper, curtain, drapes, blinds, windows, hook, mantle, speakers, decorative plate, painting, tapestry, mural. *Many other answers are possible.*

Floor Items:

Wool rug, ceramic tiles, hardwood, laminate, clay tiles, linoleum, cork, porcelain tile, polished concrete, marble, granite, limestone, under pad, bamboo, hallway runner, mat, carpet. *Many other answers are possible.*

Page 21: Backwards

1. .emoh eht fo traeh eht si nehctik ehT
2. .elbatrofmoc flesruoy ekaM
3. .ecalperif eht yb rehtag s'teL
4. !pan a rof emit s'tI

Answers

Page 22: Complete

1. Spilled
2. Dogs
3. Grain
4. Think
5. Change
6. Mother
7. Deserves
8. Broke
9. Stranger
10. Err

Page 23: Merry Matching

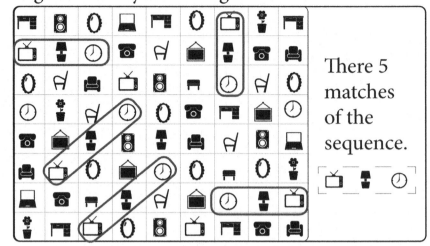

There 5 matches of the sequence.

Page 24: Sudoku

9	6	8	1	3	5	2	7	4
1	5	2	7	4	8	3	6	9
7	3	4	2	9	6	1	8	5
6	7	1	4	5	3	8	9	2
5	8	3	9	6	2	4	1	7
4	2	9	8	1	7	5	3	6
8	1	7	6	2	4	9	5	3
2	9	5	3	7	1	6	4	8
3	4	6	5	8	9	7	2	1

Pages 27-28: Challenge

1. Wall
2. Kangaroo
3. Yarn
4. Tile
5. Gum
6. Walk
7. Mail
8. Gift

Pages 25-26: Stacy's List

ottoman   (paint)   bed
curtain   tapestry   (blinds)
(lamp)   bulb   shelf
pillow   throw   hangers
(hooks)   dresser   sconce
table   (frame)   tassels
throw   (blanket)   mirror

Pages 25-26: Max's List

(chair)   cabinet   bench
(wallpaper)   mat   cart
partition   tray   (desk)
sculpture   clock   stand
bookends   stool   tray
binders   box   (rug)
(Calendar)   vase   (basket)

Page 28: Well Made Words, Letters T, P, R, M, S, O

tromps	sport	most	sort	opt	top
ports	stomp	mots	tops	pot	sop
proms	storm	port	spot	rot	*Other words*
romps	mops	post	stop	tom	*are possible.*

Pages 31-32: Particular Pictures

Page 30: Starts 'B'

1. Bracelet	5. Brooch
2. Briefcase	6. Bow tie
3. Beret	7. Boutique
4. Bathrobe	8. Birthstone

Pages 33-34: Silly Sentences

Sentence One:

A) Joyce jumps for joy when she sees emerald earrings.

Sentence Two:

D) Trevor travels with a silk scarf and a wonky watch.

Page 36: Categories

Types of Shoes:
Sandals, sneakers, pumps, hiking boots, flip flops, wedges, ballet flats, tennis shoes, running shoes, trainers, uggs, high-tops, dress shoes, slippers, stilettos and cowboy boots. *Many other answers are possible.*

Jewelry Store Items:
Ring, necklace, bracelet, brooch, pin, tiara, cuff links, watch, chain, pendant, earrings, tie clip, crystals, gold, charms, gems, beads, pearls, bangles, medallion, anklet, locket, cameo. *Many other answers are possible.*

Pages 37-38: Details

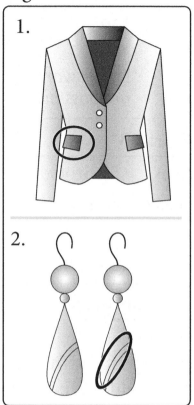

1.

2.

Page 39: 5 Differences

Page 42: Backwards

1. .revoc sti yb koob
   a egduj t'noD

2. .reven neht etal
   retteB

3. .drawrof toof tseb
   ruoy tup syawlA

4. .raet lliw thgit tub
   ,raew lliw ediW

Pages 40-41: Word Search, Winter

Page 43: Sudoku

5	6	2	3	1	7	9	4	8
4	9	1	6	8	2	5	7	3
7	8	3	9	5	4	6	1	2
9	3	6	7	2	8	4	5	1
1	2	5	4	6	9	8	3	7
8	4	7	5	3	1	2	9	6
3	7	9	2	4	6	1	8	5
2	5	8	1	9	3	7	6	4
6	1	4	8	7	5	3	2	9

Pages 45-46: Challenge

1. Ring
2. Sidewalk
3. Cookie
4. Shoe
5. Snail
6. Purse
7. Tissue
8. Truck

Page 48: Starts 'P'

1. Pottery
2. Palette
3. Pastel
4. Portrait
5. Portfolio
6. Pattern
7. Primer
8. Photograph

Page 44: Odd One Out

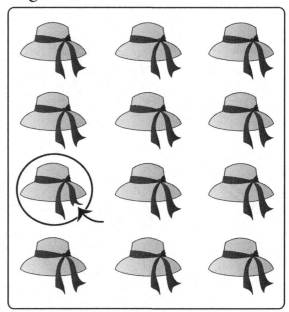

Page 46: A, L, R, K, W, E

walker	lark
waker	rale
wreak	weal
earl	war
lake	ale
leak	ear
wear	are
ware	elk
real	awe
wake	era
rake	we
weak	*Other words*
walk	*are possible.*

Answers

Pages 49-50: Particular Pictures

Pages 51-52 Silly Sentences

Sentence One:

D) Crafty Karen is gluing glitter to Ken's card

Sentence Two:

A) Henry paints a portrait of his nice niece.

Page 54: Categories

Types of Fabric:

Nylon, wool, cotton, knit, polyester, terry, linen, lycra, satin, spandex, velvet, tull, cashmere, paisley, corduroy, chino, chiffon, lace, chenille, taffeta, pashmina, jersey, neoprene. *Other answers are possible.*

Woodworking Items:

Saw, clamp, bevel, joiner, hammer, chisel, dowel, paint, primer, paint brush, sandpaper, gloves, panel, lumber, log, knife, varnish, glue, stain, wood filler, pen, wood polish, measuring tapes. *Other answers are possible.*

Page 55: Odd One Out

Page 58: Differences

Pages 56-57: Word Search, Craft

Pages 59-60: Brent's List

nails	shellac	screws
vacuum	dowel	nails
hammer	chisel	plank
pencil	level	knife
filler	paint	glue
stickers	template	board
pliers	wire	saw

Pages 59-60: Laura's List

batting	thread	tape
hoop	thimble	clips
iron	stencil	fabric
glue	pins	blade
cutter	buttons	beads
mat	scissors	lamp
tassels	fleece	ruler

Answers

Page 61: Sudoku

1	3	2	5	7	6	8	4	9
4	7	9	2	8	3	1	6	5
6	5	8	1	9	4	7	2	3
8	1	5	3	6	2	4	9	7
2	4	6	7	1	9	3	5	8
7	9	3	8	4	5	2	1	6
9	6	7	4	2	8	5	3	1
5	2	1	9	3	7	6	8	4
3	8	4	6	5	1	9	7	2

Page 62: Two of a Kind

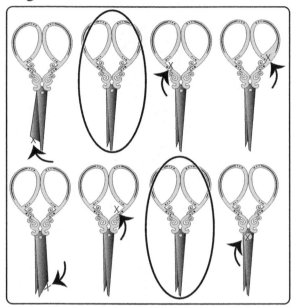

Page 64: G, I, L, N, P, A

paling	pail
align	ail
ligan	gal
aping	nip
lapin	pig
plain	lag
lain	nag
nail	lap
pane	nil
pang	*Other*
ping	*words are*
plan	*possible.*

Page 64: Challenge

1. Suit
2. Scarf
3. Milk
4. Mop
5. Paper
6. Scissors
7. Tape
8. Cup

Pages 67-68: Details

Page 66: Starts 'G'

1. Glacier	3. Green	5. Granite	7. Grizzly
2. GPS	4. Geography	6. Gravity	8. Gulf

Answers

Pages 69-70: Silly Sentences

Sentence One:
B) The lovely lake is full of feisty fish.

Sentence Two:
C) In the fabulous forest, birds sing super songs.

Pages 71-72 Particular Pictures

Page 74: Two of a Kind

Page 75: Categories

Bodies of water:
Atlantic Ocean, Pacific Ocean, Indian Ocean, Arctic Ocean, Coral Sea, Caribbean Sea, South China Sea, Mediterranean Sea, Bering Sea, Dead Sea, Lake Superior, Lake Ontario, Danube River, Nile River. *Many other answers are possible.*

Rocks & Gems:
Boulder, pebble, sand, granite, marble, limestone, sandstone, shale, amethyst, ruby, sapphire, emerald, diamond, opal, igneous, sedimentary, metamorphic, jade, chalk, soapstone. *Many other answers are possible.*

Pages 76-77: Word Search, Storms

Pages 79-80: George

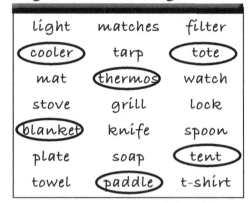

light   matches   filter
cooler   tarp   tote
mat   thermos   watch
stove   grill   lock
blanket   knife   spoon
plate   soap   tent
towel   paddle   t-shirt

Pages 79-80: Wendy

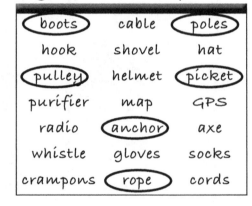

boots   cable   poles
hook   shovel   hat
pulley   helmet   picket
purifier   map   GPS
radio   anchor   axe
whistle   gloves   socks
crampons   rope   cords

Page 78: Merry Matching

There 8 matches of the sequence.

Page 81: Sudoku

7	3	9	5	2	8	6	4	1
8	2	6	4	1	3	5	7	9
5	1	4	6	9	7	8	2	3
6	9	2	7	3	1	4	5	8
1	7	5	8	6	4	9	3	2
4	8	3	2	5	9	1	6	7
2	4	1	3	8	6	7	9	5
9	5	7	1	4	2	3	8	6
3	6	8	9	7	5	2	1	4

Page 82: Odd One Out

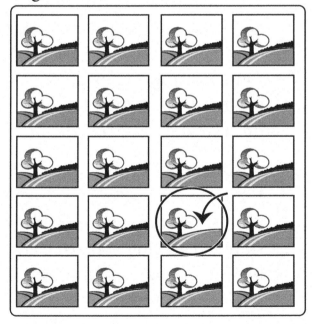

Pages 83-84: Challenge

1. Beaver	5. Grass
2. Ice cream	6. Pen
3. Lake	7. Field
4. Spoon	8. Hole

Page 84: E, O, D, R, A, F

fedora	dear
adore	fear
oared	fad
afore	doe
aero	rod
doer	are
read	for
dare	ear
redo	rad
deaf	far
fade	ode
ford	*Other words*
road	*are possible.*

Page 86: Starts 'C'

1. Camel	5. Cow
2. Crane	6. Cougar
3. Crocodile	7. Crab
4. Coyote	8. Chimpanzee

Pages 87-88: Particular Pictures

Page 93: Differences

Pages 89-90: Silly Sentences

Sentence One:
A) The delightful dog likes to eat peanut butter.

Sentence Two:
C) The wonderful walrus rests on the extra, cold ice.

Page 92: Categories

Birds:

Robin, woodpecker, starling, crow, finch, sparrow, cardinal, blue jay, dove, chickadee, pelican, loon, penguin, duck, chicken, pigeon, warbler, owl, flamingo, canary, parrot, toucan, hummingbird, eagle, black bird. *Many other answers are possible.*

Animals with Fur:

Fox, wolf, jackal, mink, rabbit, otter, raccoon, sable, skunk, cat, dog, polar bear, beaver, grizzly, muskrat, koala, chipmunk, squirrel, lemur, leopard, hare, hamster, gerbil. *Many other answers are possible.*

Pages 94-95: Word Search, Bears

Page 96: Two of a Kind

Pages 97-98: June

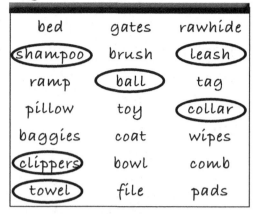

bed · gates · rawhide · shampoo · brush · leash · ramp · ball · tag · pillow · toy · collar · baggies · coat · wipes · clippers · bowl · comb · towel · file · pads

Pages 97-98: Liam

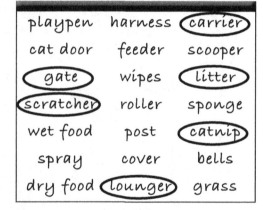

playpen · harness · carrier · cat door · feeder · scooper · gate · wipes · litter · scratcher · roller · sponge · wet food · post · catnip · spray · cover · bells · dry food · lounger · grass

Pages 99-100: Details

1.

2.

Page 102: Letters T, L, E, Y, P, A

aptly	teal	play	let
leapt	yelp	type	pat
pleat	leap	ale	pay
petal	pelt	apt	at
plate	lept	pet	*Other*
peat	tale	yet	*words are*
plea	pale	tea	*possible.*

Pages 101-102: Challenge

1. Goldfish	5. Dinosaur
2. Key	6. Rose
3. Desk	7. Water
4. Dog	8. Duck

Pages 105-106: Particular Pictures

Page 104: Starts 'T'

1. Tune	5. Tour
2. Trumpet	6. Tambourine
3. Tempo	7. Timbre
4. Tenor	8. Triangle

Page 109: Differences

Pages 107-108: Silly Sentences

Sentence One:

D) Patty plays the piccolo for a classical concert.

Sentence Two:

C) David's drumming keeps his rock band humming.

Pages 110-111: Word Search, Piano

```
W W M E L O D Y N V A L C E K R R
V D T C S O S U M P S D P L E M R
C B Q Z P F Y H M A E C A I E P E
H G U N E R M Z A O O R A G T F N
A T F D B X A I T R P K F L I C P
Y N O T E S H C N U P E Y O E O H
D V O C H O R D T O J Y Z N R L U
E W I V O R I E S I R S N X A M U
N P E D A L D T H J C G M F Y E H
B C H O P I N Y E K R E A M S E G
M J A T E C H N I Q U E J U T C W
F U P R I G H T Y M A R O R A O E
S X H H C Q X D O N D D R D C N U
O Q I H T L I S C O R E N B C C D
N F Z K U L T I M B R E P N A E U
A E D Z U S M O Z A R T Q C T R G
T E T U N E L I B E R A C E O T H
A M S T R I N G S A K U A M B O F
S V O L U K P B E E T H O V E N L
L H I O K N G R A N D G G L P B A
V O S Y V C A D E N C E L Y B X T
S I X K K V L R N T R E B L E O U
```

Page 112: Sudoku

3	7	9	2	6	4	8	1	5
6	4	8	5	1	7	3	2	9
2	1	5	9	8	3	6	7	4
8	2	3	4	9	5	7	6	1
9	5	7	1	2	6	4	8	3
1	6	4	7	3	8	5	9	2
7	3	2	6	5	9	1	4	8
4	8	1	3	7	2	9	5	6
5	9	6	8	4	1	2	3	7

Pages 113-114: Ted

8	71	4	23
10	91	6	5
62	9	11	13
7	34	82	93
46	42	14	0
1	21	73	2

Pages 113-114: Sara

32	5	92	7
96	11	72	3
81	24	5	71
9	74	62	6
64	23	17	19
76	3	8	82

Page 115: Odd One Out

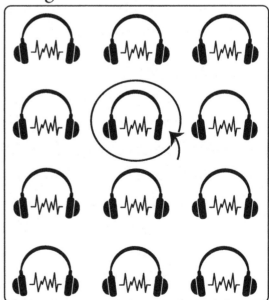

Page 116: Complete It

1. Fair	6. Mormon
2. Phantom	7. Roof
3. Beast	8. Happened
4. Bye	9. Sound
5. Business	10. Amazing

Page 117: Backwards

1. !srae ym ot cisum s'tahT
2. .lufrednow eb ot gniog si trecnoc ehT
3. .enohpoxas eht si tnemurtsni etirovaf yM
4. !ydolem ylevol a tahW

Page 118: Categories

Musical Groups:

U2, The Beatles, Queen, Green Day, Pink Floyd, Abba, The Police, The Rolling Stones, NSYNC, Nirvana, Maroon 5, Journey, The Black Eyed Peas, The Temptations, Cold Play, Pearl Jam, The Bee Gees. *Many other answers are possible.*

Solo Musical Acts:

Elvis Presley, Madonna, Elton John, Whitney Houston, Celine Dion, Garth Brooks, Billy Joel, Adele, Rod Stewart, Prince, Kenny Rogers, David Bowie, Cher, Barry White, Johnny Cash. *Many other answers are possible.*

Pages 119-120: Challenge

1. Flute	5. Guitar
2. Rabbit	6. Chair
3. Bubble	7. Sidewalk
4. Pear	8. Sandwich

Page 120: H, D, S, A, E, I

aides	dash	she
ideas	dies	ads
aside	shad	ade
heads	dis	sad
shade	his	dis
shied	has	is
dish	sea	hi
shed	hid	id
said	ash	*Other*
side	had	*words are*
ides	aid	*possible.*

Pages 122-123: Word Search, Trees

Page 124: Differences

Pages 125: Unscramble

1. Menu	5. Table
2. Waiter	6. Buffet
3. Dessert	7. Dining
4. Chef	

Page 127: Two of a Kind

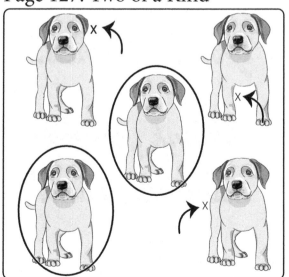

Page 126: Sudoku

8	1	2	5	6	9	7	3	4
7	5	9	4	3	1	2	6	8
6	3	4	2	8	7	1	9	5
1	6	3	9	5	2	8	4	7
4	9	5	6	7	8	3	1	2
2	8	7	3	1	4	6	5	9
5	4	1	7	2	6	9	8	3
3	2	6	8	9	5	4	7	1
9	7	8	1	4	3	5	2	6

Page 128: Odd One Out

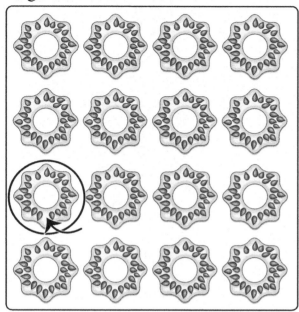

Pages 129-130: Details

Page 131: Shadow Finder

Well Done!

You've finished.

Thank you for using this book!

Made in United States
North Haven, CT
09 October 2021

10224606R00085